Animals

Armed for Survival

Stanford Makishi

Contents

Rigby

A Harcourt Achieve Imprint

www.Rigby.com
1-800-531-5015

What is armor?

Have you ever seen an armored car on the street or a suit of armor in a museum? Armor is a kind of metal covering that protects a person or thing.

Presidents and other leaders ride in armored cars for their protection. An armored car has a super-strong body that protects the people or expensive things inside it. Many businesses hire armored trucks to drive their money safely to the bank.

armored truck

Can you imagine wearing a heavy suit of armor? Until the 1500s that's what fighters wore in battle. Human armor included a helmet, suit, and shoes made of metal. If a sword came crashing down, the armor protected the person inside. Fighters even put armor on their dogs!

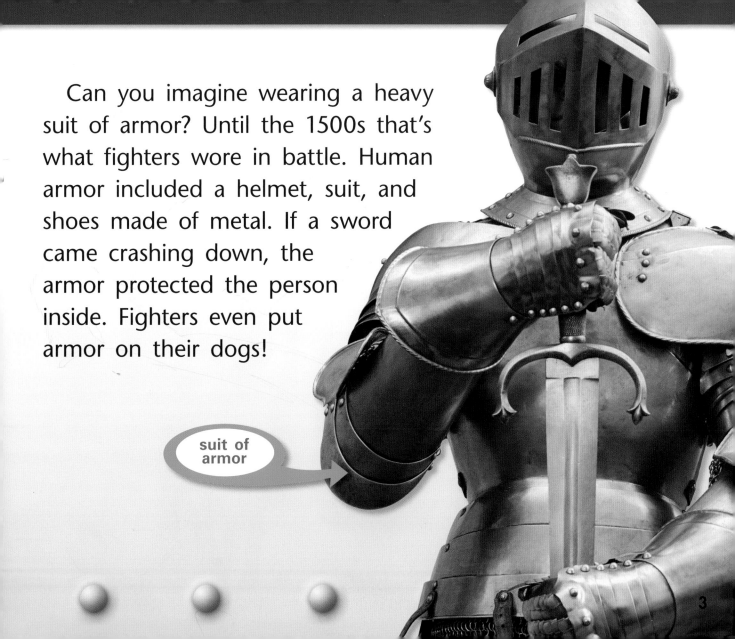

suit of armor

How can a wild animal have armor?

Animals in the wild must protect themselves from other animals, harsh weather, and even humans. Many animals run to escape danger. Some animals use poison to protect themselves. Other animals flock together or stay in large herds for protection.

armored lobster

The colorful armor on this beetle's back helps protect it.

Of course, no animal is made of metal. However, many wild creatures use their hard shells, thick skin, and tough scales to protect themselves. All these coverings work like armor to help the animals stay alive in the wild.

5

How does a turtle use its armor?

A turtle has a hard shell that it uses like armor. When it is in danger, it can hide by pulling its head, tail, and legs inside its shell. When it does this, the softer parts of its body are protected inside the hard shell.

The flesh inside the shell of a turtle is soft and needs protection. So when a turtle is hiding inside its shell, only the strong shell shows on the outside.

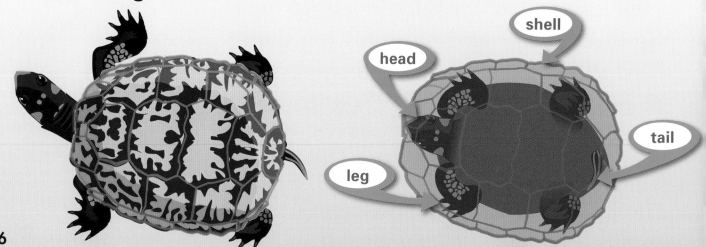

Turtles have hard shells that act like armor.

How does an armadillo use its armor?

If you've ever seen an armadillo, you know that it has amazing armor. The front and back ends of the armadillo are protected with a solid shell. The middle section is covered in bones that are held together in a striped pattern. One kind of armadillo can even roll itself up into a tight ball.

The three-banded armadillo is the only armadillo that can roll into a ball.

This armadillo shell has a striped pattern.

The armadillo's shell also keeps its body warm in winter in its home underground. In the summer, the armadillo stays cool by looking for food at night. When it's boiling hot outside, armadillos enjoy cooling off with a mud bath!

How does a porcupine use its armor?

A porcupine has an unusual coat of armor that's not made out of shell, skin, or scales. The porcupine is covered in quills. Quills are special hairs that are like long, sharp needles. These hairs have pointed tips at the ends. A porcupine can have as many as 30,000 quills.

Some people think the porcupine shoots its quills like arrows, but it doesn't. When a porcupine senses danger nearby, it first turns its back on the possible enemy. Then it swings its tail from side to side. When its tail hits the animal, the porcupine's quills stick into that animal.

The porcupine uses its armor of quills to keep enemies away.

How does a pangolin use its armor?

The pangolin looks a little like an armadillo because it also has armor. The body of a pangolin is covered in hard scales. When another animal is bothering it, the pangolin will coil itself into a ball.

Like the armadillo, the pangolin can roll itself into a ball of armor.

A pangolin uses its armored tail to protect itself.

The pangolin protects itself in another way, too. It can fight by swinging its tail. The sharp scales on its tail can be quite harmful!

How do a rhinoceros and an alligator use their armor?

The rhinoceros is really big and strong. An adult rhinoceros can grow to 6 feet tall and 15 feet long. The armor on a rhinoceros is its very thick skin. However, the large horn at the end of a rhinoceros's nose is the strongest part of its armor.

Rhinos have a tough skin that acts like armor.

Alligators are protected by their hard scales.

The alligator is a big animal with very thick skin. It's covered in hard scales, which protect it from being wounded. Its powerful jaws, sharp teeth, speed in the water, and huge size also protect the alligator. Plus, the alligator can grow to be 15 feet long. That's about the size of a minivan!

All these wild animals have heavy armor to protect themselves. So unless you're wearing armor, too, you had better keep your distance!

Index